Stepping Through History

WRITING

PEGGY BURNS

Thomson Learning • New York

Stepping Through History

The Mail
Money
News
Stores and Markets
Travel
Writing

First published in the United States in 1995 by
Thomson Learning
115 Fifth Avenue
New York, NY 10003

First published in Great Britain in 1995 by Wayland (Publishers) Ltd.

Library of Congress Cataloging-in-Publication Data
Burns, Peggy.
Writing / Peggy Burns.
    p.   cm.—(Traditions around the world)
Includes index.
  ISBN 1-56847-341-9
1. Writing—History—Juvenile literature.
[1. Writing—History]
I. Title. II. Series
Z40.B86   1995
5411—dc20   94-36116

Printed in Italy

Picture Acknowledgments

The Publishers would like to thank the following for allowing their pictures to be used in this book:
Ann Ronan 15, 16 (above), 17, 22 (below), 27, 28 (above); British Telecom Museum 13 (Imperial War Museum); Eye Ubiquitous 5; Image Select 23 (below); Mary Evans **contents,** 12, 19, 28 (below); Michael Holford **cover** (top), 4, 5 (above), 6, 7, 8 (below), 9, 14; Robert Harding 11; Parker Pens Ltd 20, 21 (below), 22 (above); Ronald Sheridan 10, 18, 24 (below), 26 (below); The Science Museum 24 (above); Tony Stone 11, 29; Wayland Picture Library **cover** (right and left), *title,* 16 (left), 19 (below), 23 (above), *time line* (top: Biblioteca Laurenzia), *time line* (middle: British Museum), *time line* (bottom), Werner Forman 8 (above), 25, 26 (above).

CONTENTS

Words in *bold italic* in the main text are explained in the glossary on page 31.

WORDS IN PICTURES

Writing is such an important part of our lives. Without it we would have difficulty remembering all that we learn; we would not have accurate records of all the information that is necessary to carry on our lives.

Early Stone Age people very soon realized the need to communicate beyond the spoken word. From simple sounds and gestures that were used to name objects and share feelings, there evolved systems of depicting and recording what people thought and what they needed to keep track of. Farmers, for example, needed to keep records of crops and animals, and people needed to count off the days, weeks, and years.

The very beginnings of writing consisted of using available materials, such a bone and stone. With these primitive writing implements messages were written on rocks and cave walls. Natural dyes were also used to draw pictures of animals and people involved with their daily lives. These earliest forms of writing, dating from about 30,000 B.C., were geometric shapes which show people and animals. These are known as pictographs. A simple pictograph message might look like this:

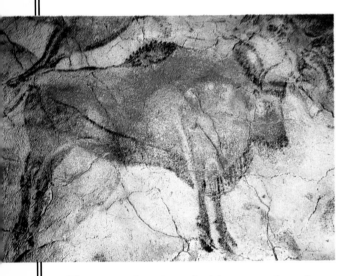

This cave drawing of a bison was found in northern Spain. It was drawn by cave dwellers over 14,000 years ago.

Pictographs could be used to keep records. This ancient tablet from Mesopotamia (now in modern-day Turkey) is a farming record, showing where crops were grown.

This would tell the person reading it, "I am going to the woods to hunt. Back tonight."

You can seen pictographs all around you today. They are still very useful ways of conveying information. For instance, a stick figure shown on a door represents a public restroom. Road symbol signs are modern-day pictographs that provide warnings of what lies ahead on the road, such as a curved road or an upcoming intersection.

One advantage of pictographs is that they can be understood even by people who can't read the language of the country or area in which they are staying.

This Australian road sign is a modern pictograph. It warns that kangaroos may be crossing the road.

THE FIRST WRITTEN LANGUAGE

This tablet from Sumeria was engraved with pictographs around 5,000 years ago. The earliest known written language was called "cuneiform" and developed from pictographs.

The Sumerians, an ancient people who lived in Mesopotamia (between the valleys of the Tigris and Euphrates rivers in the Middle East), were the first known people to invent a written language. Around 5,000 years ago, they began to draw pictographs with reed styli (square-ended writing tools), on wet clay. The clay tablets were then hardened in the hot sun or baked in ovens to preserve the drawings. The Sumerians sometimes drew pictographs on stone or metal instead of on clay.

Over a period of many years the pictographs changed as people began to use symbols instead of the original, careful drawings. By 3000 B.C. the Sumerians were using wedge-shaped writing called cuneiform ("cuneus" means "wedge" in Latin). Cuneiform was quicker and easier to write than pictographs.

At first, there was a vast number of symbols, over 2,000 in all. As time went on the number of symbols was reduced to around 800, of which 200 to 300 were commonly used. The symbols also could be used to write different languages.

This Sumerian statue was carved with cuneiform writing in 860 B.C.

IDEAS, SOUNDS, AND ALPHABETS

The ancient Egyptians lived in the Nile Valley between 5,000 and 6,000 years ago. Around 3000 B.C. they invented hieroglyphs – symbols that stood for letters, words, and ideas. Like cuneiform, these symbols also developed from pictographs.

Many of the symbols were pictures of animals, birds, and people and are recognizable today. Others stood for single sounds, but most Egyptian hieroglyphs stood for ideas. A picture of an eye with a tear coming from it was not the word "eye;" it meant "sorrow." Idea symbols are known as ideograms.

Hieroglyphs were carved on limestone tablets. These hieroglyphs date back to 1400 B.C.

The Rosetta Stone.

For many years hieroglyphs could not be understood. Then in 1799, in Egypt, a key discovery was made. A large stone slab—the Rosetta Stone—was found that bore an inscription in three different written languages: Greek, hieroglyphs, and another Egyptian script called "demotic."

A French scholar, Jean-François Champollion, used the Greek, which he could understand, to translate the meaning of hieroglyphs for the first time. However, because the ancient Egyptian language was not a true alphabet but was mainly written in ideograms, we will never know what it sounded like when spoken.

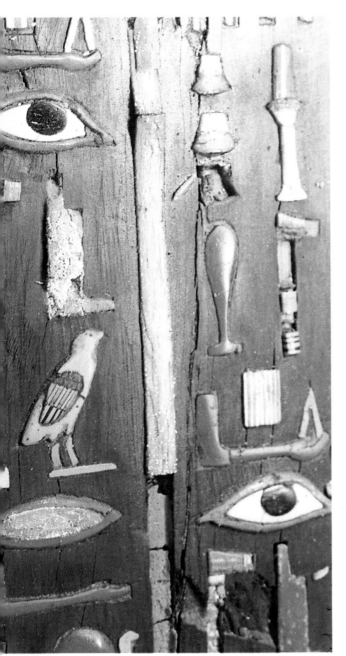

Left: These Egyptian hieroglyphs from the fourth century B.C. decorated the inside of an Egyptian wooden coffin.

This child is learning calligraphy at the Shanghai Palace of Culture in China. Writing Chinese characters is very difficult and takes many years to learn.

The Chinese began to create their own writing system about 1500 B.C. Chinese writing developed using a combination of pictographs, ideograms, and symbols representing sounds. It has changed little over time, and today young Chinese learn to read ancient as well as modern Chinese writing.

Each Chinese character stands for a whole word, so many thousands of characters are needed to write down the language. In all there are over 40,000 characters compared to the 26 letters in the Roman alphabet. Not all the characters are used in everyday life. A Chinese child will learn an average of 4,000 characters during the years he or she is at school. Some characters need as many as 32 strokes of the pen. It is not surprising that writing Chinese is considered an art form.

Western languages are written using an alphabet. An alphabet is different from pictographs or ideograms. Each letter of the alphabet stands for a particular sound. Letters are combined to make words. You can write down the letters C, A, and T, and sound them out to make the word "cat."

The Phoenicians, who lived along the coast of Syria and Israel around 1800 B.C., were the first people to have the idea of using letters to represent sounds. Using a mixture of symbols from earlier writing systems, they devised letters for the first true alphabet around 1050 B.C.

The Phoenicians were great traders and sailors and their language spread with their travels around the world. Today's Greek, Arabic, and Hebrew scripts, the Cyrillic alphabet used in Russia, and the Roman alphabet, which is used to write many of the world's languages including English, all can be traced back to the ancient script of the Phoenicians.

The Roman alphabet descended from the early Phoenician alphabet.

CODES AND SHORTHAND

There are ways to write down languages other than using alphabets, pictographs, or ideograms. Examples include shorthand, braille, and secret codes.

Shorthand is a way of writing words and sentences very rapidly using abbreviations. The ancient Greeks developed a kind of shorthand but its use faded out during Roman times.

There were several important contributions to shorthand during the seventeeth century. But the Gregg system, introduced to the United States in 1893 by Irish-born John Robert Gregg, became the most widely used system in the U.S.

All writing systems have relied on visual signs to communicate language. However, a system to enable *visually impaired* people to read was invented in France in 1824 by Louis Braille. Braille, who had been blinded in an accident at the age of three, created an amazing system of small raised dots that stood for numbers, letters of the alphabet, and even music. The dots, punched into a page of thick paper, could be felt with the fingertips. Braille writing opened up a whole new world to visually impaired people.

This magazine cover shows shorthand being used. A skilled shorthand journalist can write down up to 120 words a minute.

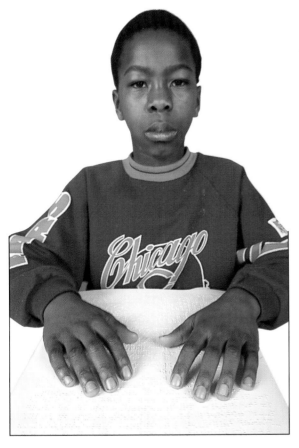

Above: This visually impaired boy is reading braille by touch, through his fingers.

The great advantage of writing is that it can be understood by other people, but sometimes this is a disadvantage if you want to keep information secret. Messages during wartime need to be kept secret from the enemy. Coded messages were widely used during World War I to pass on sensitive information. Often the codes were disguised in letters or messages that would not appear suspicious to anyone else. Letters to relatives, grocery orders, and delivery notes often contained secret information passed on in code.

During World War I, wartime messages were sent by code in order to keep information secret from the enemy.

HOW PAPER WAS INVENTED

Ancient Egyptians made the earliest form of paper from the papyrus reeds that grew along the banks of the Nile River. The oldest surviving papyrus was made more than 5,000 years ago.

Thin sheets were made from the stems of the papyrus plant, which were then wetted, pressed flat, and dried in the sun. Scribes glued sheets of papyrus together into long lengths, then rolled them up into a scroll, ready to be written on.

The advantage of papyrus was that there was a plentiful supply of reeds available. Plantations were set up and run by the ancient Egyptian rulers. Papyrus was expensive, so it was reserved for important documents such as religious scriptures and legal documents.

The holy book of the ancient Egyptians, the *Book of the Dead*, was written on papyrus around 1250 B.C.

Trade with other nations spread the use of Egyptian papyrus to countries all around the Mediterranean. The demand for papyrus was huge. Egyptian supplies could not always be relied on outside Egypt. A suitable alternative was found in parchment, which could be produced anywhere.

The ancient Chinese made paper by cutting bamboo (left), soaking it in water, and then pounding it to a pulp. After soaking with lime, the pulp was drained and dried and the new sheet of paper trimmed (right).

It is said that parchment was invented by King Eumenes II when papyrus was in short supply during his reign (197 to c. 160 B.C.). The word parchment comes from the name of his kingdom, Pergamum (now in modern-day Turkey). Parchment was made from animal skins, washed in water and lime, and then stretched on a frame. Although papyrus was still being used by the Romans in A.D. 273, parchment was the main writing material used in Europe until the sixteenth century.

In A.D 105, a Chinese man, Ts'ai Lun, soaked grass, leaves, bark, and old rags in lime water until they turned to pulp. He strained the mixture through a sieve and pressed it into flat sheets of paper. Later, the bark of mulberry trees (or *bamboo*) was used instead of the original soaked grass used by Ts'ai Lun. This made a high quality white paper that became popular because it was cheaper to produce than the silk on which the Chinese had been writing.

For almost 700 years the Chinese kept the secret of papermaking to themselves. It was not until some papermakers were taken prisoner by Muslim invaders that the secret was passed on in return for their freedom. By 1400, there were paper mills in Spain, France, and Italy. In 1690, the first American paper mill opened in Pennsylvania.

At first paper was very expensive. Until the nineteenth century, paper was handmade. One of the earliest paper-making machines was invented in 1798 in France. Paper became cheaper as more paper mills opened, and pulped wood began to be used.

Paper mills in the seventeenth century were powered by waterwheels.

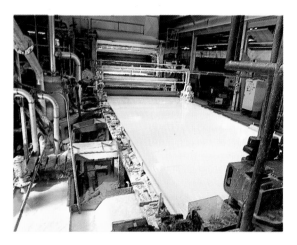

Part of a modern papermaking machine where the pulp is soaked in water.

Today, there are many types of paper, such as *paperboard*, tracing paper, wax paper, newsprint, and wrapping papers. Wood and other natural fibers, such as cotton rags, are ground up and mixed with water. This pulp is then heated in chemicals and washed and mixed with other substances that improve the quality of the paper. Presses squeeze most of the water from the wet pulp, and the newly formed paper is then dried and wound into huge rolls. The machines that make these rolls can be a half a mile or more in length.

EARLY WRITING TOOLS

Ancient civilizations had no pens or pencils as we know them today. People used materials they found around them, such as clay, bone, reeds, stone, or tree bark, to handcraft writing tools. Even sharks' teeth were used by the people of Easter Island in the Pacific.

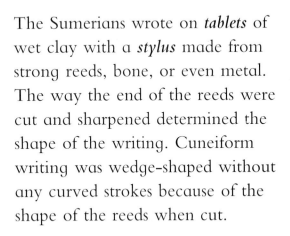

A drawing of a stylus and clay tablet.

The Sumerians wrote on *tablets* of wet clay with a *stylus* made from strong reeds, bone, or even metal. The way the end of the reeds were cut and sharpened determined the shape of the writing. Cuneiform writing was wedge-shaped without any curved strokes because of the shape of the reeds when cut.

Ancient Egyptians wrote hieroglyphs on temple walls with brushes made from thin strands of papyrus. Later, reed pens and brushes were used to write in ink on papyrus. Black ink was made from carbon and water for the first time. The reeds were split at the end to help the ink flow, in a similiar way to a modern fountain pen nib.

The early writing tools in China called "pi" were used to write in dark varnish or ink on bone, bamboo, and silk. "Pi" brushes were made of animal hair secured with silk thread to wooden handles.

A man and woman from Roman times holding a stylus, tablet, and papyrus scroll.

Above: A Roman stylus and writing tablet. The wooden tablet was covered in wax which was then written on.

Ancient Romans wrote with iron or bronze styli on papyrus, parchment, or on wooden tablets covered with wax. Wax-covered tablets were commonly used because the writing could be rubbed out and the wax could be written on again.

The first pencils were invented by the Romans. These were simply flat cakes of lead that were used to rule faint guidelines on stone ready for carving.

Around A.D. 600, quill pens made from the strong flight feathers of a goose or other large bird began to be used in Europe. The hard tip of the feather was cut into a writing point and the natural hollow within the feather helped to hold the ink. Goose feathers were particularly suitable for quills because of the way they curve. The feathers on each wing curve in opposite directions. The feathers from a left wing are best suited to right-handed people and those from the right wing to left-handed people.

Pencils as we know them today were first introduced in France, in 1795. A wooden case was glued around a stick of *graphite* and clay. This helped to keep the writer's hand clean. The great advantage of pencil is that it can be erased.

In the same way, children in the nineteenth century used chalk on slates to do their schoolwork because it could be rubbed out easily. However, writing in chalk or pencil is not as long lasting as writing done in ink.

This advertisement from 1927 encouraged people to buy Zeus pencils. Zeus pencils were made in Austria.

For around 1200 years the quill pen remained the most popular writing tool in Europe. As late as the mid-nineteenth century, quill pens were still being used to write with in homes, schools, and offices. But feathers tended to wear out quickly, and cutting new pens took time and skill. A more durable pen than the quill was needed.

PEN AND INK

In 1748, Johann Janssen, an inventor from Aachen in Germany, created the first writing point made from steel. Others quickly followed, and inventors in France and Germany also claimed to have made the first steel pen.

In the early days, metal writing points, or nibs, were made by hand from thin strips of metal. The metal was hammered into a tube shape that fitted over the end of a wooden holder, then the writing tip was filed to a point. These proved to be very popular and by 1830, steel pen nibs were being produced by steam-powered machines in factories.

The invention of the steel pen nib brought about other changes. It was found that the ink that had been used with quill pens caused the new metal pens to rust. Inventors had to experiment with new inks. Some of them deteriorated quickly and had a bad odor. Advances in chemistry and the invention of new dyes, however, soon improved the quality of ink.

Steel pens were an improvement on quills, but they had drawbacks. The writer had to keep dipping his or her pen into an inkwell.

A modern pen nib being cut by a machine.

HOW EARLY INKS WERE MADE

Ink has been used since ancient times and was usually made of soot from oil lamps mixed with resin, gum, honey, borax, burned almonds, or even cows' urine. In ancient Egypt and China, black or red ink was often made in solid disks or sticks, much like the solid paint in artists' palettes today. From Roman times until the nineteenth century, European ink was made from oak galls – growths on oak twigs made by insects – mixed with iron salts.

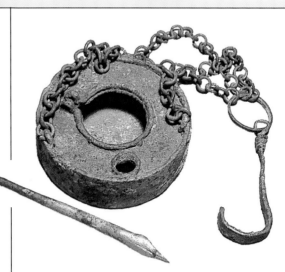

A Roman pen and inkwell made from bronze.

The first *fountain pen* may have been made as far back as the tenth century, when the Arab leader Caliph al-Mu'izz demanded a pen with its own supply of ink. His craftsmen made one for him from gold—but no one knows how well it worked. Fountain pens were reinvented in the 1880s, but they were not very good. Ink did not flow out smoothly.

Modern pens.

George S. Parker, the founder of the Parker Pen Company.

One of the first manufacturers of the modern pen was George S. Parker, a lecturer who worked on improving the fountain pens supplied to his students. He started the Parker Pen Company, and by the end of the 1930s, he was the world leader of the fountain pen industry.

Although there were earlier attempts, Laszlo Biro, a Hungarian, invented the first efficient ballpoint pen in 1943. Today, the ballpoint pen is still known as a "biro" in Great Britain. Ballpoint pens differ from fountain pens in that they encase a tiny ball at the tip of the pen. As the writer moves the pen across the page the ball rolls and the ink, contained in a narrow plastic tube, is gently released onto the page.

In America, businessman Middleton Reynolds got the U.S. patent for Biro's pen. It was reported that nearly ten thousand of Middleton's pens were sold in a single day at one store.

An advertisement for ballpoint pens dated 1888. Early ballpoint pens did not write very well.

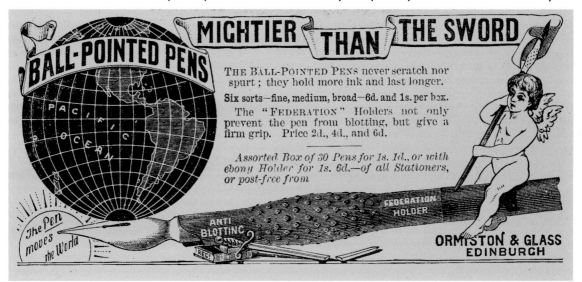

EARLY PRINTING

Before printing was invented books had to be written by hand. *Scribes* could take many months or even years to produce a single handwritten book. This made books very valuable. Many books were written and bound for the Christian Church by monks and nuns. *Illuminated manuscripts* from *medieval* times are among the most beautifully illustrated books in the world.

An illustration from a medieval manuscript. Here a monk takes a drink of ale.

More than a thousand years ago, the Chinese found out how to print using carved blocks of wood. Each wooden block had a whole page of characters on it.

Later, around A.D. 1045, the Chinese developed movable type made from pottery. This could be used to print characters in different arrangements over and over again.

By 1400, Europeans were printing with inked, wooden blocks just as the Chinese had done over 700 years earlier. A German goldsmith, Johannes Gutenberg, produced the first printing press in the town of Mainz in 1455.

The first printed Bible produced by Gutenberg contained over 1,200 pages.

Right: This eighteenth-century printing press is similiar to Gutenberg's original design.

The press was operated by hand and used metal type. Metal letters were arranged into words and sentences, then locked together within a frame. Ink was spread thinly over the surface, and paper was then pressed down on it to print a page of a book.

The *mechanical* printing press was invented in 1477. The idea spread rapidly and for the next 300 years printing presses changed little from Gutenberg's original design.

The first printers tried to imitate the handwritten style of the scribes and even had illuminated initial letters and handwritten decoration put on the pages. It took many years for printers to develop the modern *typefaces* of today.

JOHANNES GUTENBERG

Johannes Gutenberg ran into trouble with his partner, Johannes Fust. Fust, who had provided the money for the press, became impatient with delays in starting up the press. He won a lawsuit against Gutenberg only days before the first books were due to be published in 1456. Gutenberg lost his equipment, and the first books printed on his press bore the name of Fust only. Other people made a fortune from Gutenberg's ideas, but the inventor himself was better at inventing than he was at business.

An engraving of Johannes Gutenberg.

MAKING BOOKS

The *Diamond Sutra*—the earliest known printed book—was produced in China in A.D. 868. Printed on it was a Buddhist prayer with intricate artwork designed around it.

The Buddha design was printed on a separate sheet of paper and then glued to the text in the form of a scroll. The scroll is over 15 feet in length. It is very different from the bound books of today.

The *Diamond Sutra* was printed using seven different printing blocks made of wood.

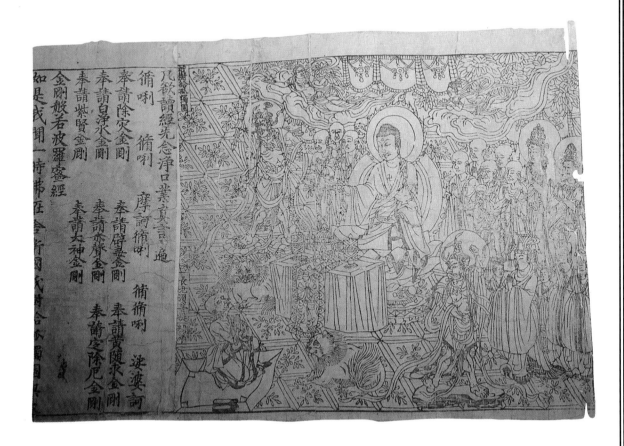

This codex comes from Mexico. The Aztecs (the ancient people of Central America) made it from beaten deer skin.

We owe the shape and form of books to the Romans. The Romans began to fold squares of parchment into sheets and sew them together on one side. This was better than scrolls because both sides could be written on. These early books, called *codices,* were widely used by A.D. 400.

William Caxton set up the first printing press in London in 1476. Caxton is famous for printing the first Bible in English, but he also printed novels, romances, and educational books. In 1639, Stephen Daye set up the first printing press in America in Cambridge, Massachusetts.

This Bible is known as the Lindisfarne Gospels. It was handwritten and bound in England in the year A.D. 698.

Binding of books is important to protect the pages from damage.

MODERN DEVELOPMENTS

By 1814 a steam-powered printing press could produce 1,100 printed sheets an hour. However, the workers setting type by hand could only set 2,000 letters an hour, which held up the printing process.

American inventors developed faster ways of setting type by machine. Monotype machines set type letter by letter and linotype machines set a whole line of type in one operation. Linotype machines, introduced in 1886 in New York, could set over 6,000 letters an hour (three times as fast as by hand).

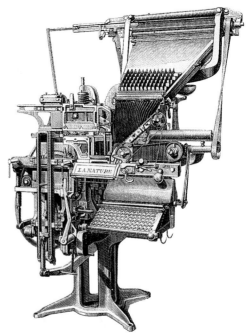

Above: A Linotype typesetting or "composing" machine made in 1893.

This steam-powered rotary printing press was invented in 1818.

In 1867 an American, C. Latham Sholes, invented the first real typewriter. Earlier typewriters had been patented, but were not very good or useful. Sholes' machine was later marketed by the Remington Company, becoming popular in offices and homes throughout the world.

At first the typewriters were manual, which made them slow and heavy to use. By the 1950s and 1960s, electric typewriters had become common in offices. A fast typist could type more than 75 words a minute. Today, typing is usually done on computers.

A drawing of the first typewriter invented by C. Latham Sholes in 1867.

This Yost typewriter was made in 1912. It was a great improvement on earlier typewriters because it was much smaller and easier to use.

Early computers, such as the *ENIAC*, were so big that they had to be set up in warehouses. They were not like the portable personal computers of today, some of which are small enough to fit inside a briefcase. Computers have now become vital to the smooth running of businesses and governments. A large *database* can store millions of pieces of written information that can be accessed by telephone via *modems* from anywhere in the world.

INFORMATION TECHNOLOGY

Information technology has entirely revolutionized newspaper and book production. In newsrooms, writers enter their stories directly onto a computer using a video display terminal. When finished, a push of a button sends the information to the main computer where it is processed, ready to be printed.

Telephones and *fiber optics* are making it possible to pass information at the speed of light (around 186,282 miles per second) around the world. Because of this *The Financial Times* and *Wall Street Journal* newspapers are able to print newspaper editions in a number of different countries at the same time.

This author is working at a video display terminal, more commonly known as a VDT.

TIME LINE

c. 30,000 B.C. Stone Age people begin to paint pictures on cave walls.	**3500 B.C.** The Sumerian people start to use pictographs as writing.	**3000 B.C.** Cuneiform writing evolves from pictographs in Mesopotamia.	**3000 B.C.** The ancient Egyptians develop hieroglyphs.	**1500 B.C.** The Chinese develop a writing system based on pictographs.

A.D. 105 In China paper is invented by Ts'ai Lun.	**A.D. 200** The Chinese invent printing using carved wooden blocks.	**A.D. 400** Early books or codices are widely used by the Romans instead of scrolls.		**A.D. 1041** The Chinese develop movable type.

1151 Papermaking begins in Europe.		**1400** In Europe printing with carved wooden blocks replaces handwritten manuscripts.	**1455** In Germany Johannes Gutenberg invents the first printing press using movable metal type.	**1476** William Caxton sets up the first printing press in England.

1456 First books printed on Gutenberg's mechanical printing press.	**1748** The first steel pen is invented by Johann Janssen in Germany.		**1811** The steam-powered printing press is invented.	**1824** Louis Braille invents the braille system of writing for the visually impaired.

1867 An American, C. Latham Sholes, invents the first typewriter.	**1880s** The first efficient fountain pens are made.	**1886** Type is set by machine on Monotype and Linotype machines.	**1940s** Computers are invented. The first efficient ballpoint pen is invented.	**1980s** Typesetting machines are no longer needed as computers transform print production.

GLOSSARY

Bamboo A plant with hollow woody stems that grows in hot countries.

Codex (Codices) An early book with the pages stitched together down one side.

Database Files on computer, storing many records of information, organized for rapid search and retrieval. Magazines, for example, often keep names and addresses of their subscribers on a database.

ENIAC Considered one of the first modern computers. The name means Electronic Numerical Integrator and Calculator.

Fiber optics Fine, flexible glass strands that send messages using light.

Fountain Pen A type of pen with ink inside it that flows out so the writer does not have to dip the pen into an inkwell.

Graphite A type of carbon that is gray and can be used to write with.

Illuminated manuscripts Books that were hand-produced in medieval times. They were ornately illustrated, or "illuminated."

Information technology Speech, text, and visual information fed into computers to be processed.

Mechanical Using machine power instead of doing something by hand.

Medieval The period of history between the fifth and fifteenth centuries A.D.

Modem The hookup that enables computers to work be connected through telephone lines.

Paperboard Thick paper similiar to cardboard used to cover books.

Scribes People whose job it was to write out books and scrolls by hand.

Stylus (styli) A pointed writing tool made out of metal or reed plants.

Tablet A small, flat piece of wood or stone used to write on.

Typeface Design of letters and symbols used in printing.

Visually impaired A person with damaged or weakened eyesight.

BOOKS TO READ

Aliki. *Communication*. New York: Greenwillow Books, 1993.

Benjamin, Carol L. *Writing for Kids*. New York: HarperCollins Children's Books, 1985.

Cobb, Vicki. *Writing It Down*. New York: HarperCollins Children's Books, 1989.

Fisher, Leonard E. *Gutenberg*. New York: Macmillan Children's Book Group, 1993.

Suhr, Mandy. *Making a Book*. New York: Thomson Learning, 1994.

Watts, L. and Inglis, L. *Computers*. Young Scientist. Tulsa, OK: EDC 1993.

Merlyn's Pen (A magazine that publishes kids' writing and artwork)
Box 1058
East Greenwich, RI 02818

INDEX

Numbers in **bold** indicate subjects shown in pictures as well as in the text.